On the wind

T0372054

Dan, Sam and Nat are at the park. There is a lot of wind.

Nat likes running with the wind in her hair. Pam likes it too.

Sam is looking at a man
wind surfing. The wind is
helping him a lot.

Dan is standing by the pond. He is clinging on tight to the string.

An old man tips his hat and says to Dan, "That's a good thing to do today."

All of a sudden, a big gust of wind lifts the man's wig up!

The man puts his hat back on and keeps going.

The wig drifts up into the air.
It drifts up higher and higher.

The kids see the
wig and run to it.

The wig flaps up high
on the wind and then
lands on a twig.

It looks like it is stuck there.
But then a robin jumps out of
her nest. She pecks at the wig

When the wig drops off
the twig, it is swept off
by the wind.

Then it flops back
down and the kids
attempt to grab it.

But then a big puff of
wind picks it up and it is
off. It is now out of sight.

The old man comes back.
"Have you kids seen my
wig?" he says.

Words to blend

park	hair	air
too	looking	good
looks	surfing	tight
higher	high	see
down	clinging	nest
attempt	wind	twig
pond	flaps	lands

Before reading

Synopsis: Dan, Nat and Sam are at the park on a windy day. When a man there loses something, they go and try to find it for him.

Review graphemes/phonemes: ar air oo ur igh ee ow

Story discussion: Look at the cover, and read the title together. Ask: *Where are the children? What is the weather like? What do you think will happen in this story?*

Link to prior learning: Display a word with adjacent consonants from the story, e.g. *string*. Ask children to put a dot under each single-letter grapheme (s, t, r, i) and a line under the digraph (*ng*). Model, if necessary, how to sound out and blend the adjacent consonants together to read the word. Repeat with another word from the story, e.g. *drifts*, and encourage the children to sound out and blend the word independently.

Vocabulary check: wind surfing – a water sport that is like a combination of surfing and sailing. Show children the picture of the wind surfer on page 4 and talk about what he is doing.

Decoding practice: Write these words on cards: *drop, jump, flap, gust, grab*. Hold up one card at a time for children to read. Encourage fluent reading on sight, without overt sounding out and blending, as far as possible.

Tricky word practice: Display the word *today* and ask children to circle the tricky parts of the word (o, which makes a long /oo/ sound, and *ay*, which makes a long /ai/ sound). Practise writing and reading this word.

After reading

Apply learning: Ask: *Can you explain how the man's wig got back to him in the end?* (It ended up on Pam's head and she ran back with it.)

Comprehension

- Why did the man take his hat off?

- Who tried to help the man get his wig back?

- How do you think the man felt at the end of the story?

Fluency

- Pick a page that most of the group read quite easily. Ask them to reread it with pace and expression. Model how to do this if necessary.

- In pairs, children could read pages 6–7, with one child reading the old man's words and the other reading the rest of the text. Can they make their reading sound natural and fluent?

- Practise reading the words on page 17.

Tricky words review

puts	are	her
by	into	out
she	today	have
you	my	like
comes	when	the